A CENTURY of
WOLVERHAMPTON

Every Wulfrunian can tell a story. Charles and Elsie Bennett, the children of Sylvanus Bennett, Works Foreman in the Borough Engineers Department. Sylvanus was killed in October 1917 when a joist fell on his head while he was installing the temporary dance floor in the town's second-class swimming baths (see page 41). Charles was sent to the Royal School – hence the uniform. He later became Head of Accounts at the Courtaulds factory. (*Phil Bennett Collection*)

A CENTURY of

WOLVERHAMPTON

NED WILLIAMS

First published in 1999 by Sutton Publishing Limited

This new paperback edition first published in 2007 by Sutton Publishing

Reprinted in 2011 by
The History Press,
The Mill, Brimscombe Port,
Stroud, Gloucestershire, GL5 2QG
www.thehistorypress.co.uk

British Library Cataloguing in Publication Data
A catalogue record for this book is available from the British Library.

ISBN 978-0-7509-4942-2

Front endpaper: An aerial view of Wolverhampton town centre, *c.* 1949. (*Simon Dewey Collection*)
Back endpaper: A view of Queen Square, August 1996. The Square has featured in many of the photographs used in this book, and was frequently the subject of postcards sold in the town. The never-ending changes to the townscape of Queen Square are always a reflection of what is going on in the town generally. (*Ned Williams*)
Half title page: W.H. Smith & Son in Lichfield Street, 1930s. (*Author's Collection*)
Title page: Miss Winifred Irene Bennett (centre) becomes the St Luke's Church May Queen, *c.* 1912. (*Phil Bennett Collection*)

Typeset in 11/14pt Photina.
Typesetting and origination by
Sutton Publishing.
Printed and bound in England.

Contents

Above: Although Wolves football team are the most famous sporting institution associated with Wolverhampton, the Cricket Club is older – with a history stretching back to 1835! In 1973 the club's team won the Robins Trophy at Lords against The Mote. With a sense of making history they have won the trophy again in 1999! Captain David Barnes hoists the trophy aloft with his 1973 winning team – Nick Stroudley, Don Lowe, Jim Turner, Nick Marsh, Gerry Hill, Don Crofts, John Moore, Julian Pandya, Mike Marcus, Geoff Hopkinson and Peter Evans, seven of who returned in 1999. (*Express & Star*)

Left: Wolverhampton Cricket Club Captain, David Barnes, receives a bat as his award for winning the Robins (National Knockout) Trophy at Lords in 1973. Each team member received a bat from the West Indies Captain, Clive Lloyd, watched by Aidan Crawley, President of the MCC, and the sponsor Derrick Robins. (*Photo: Roy Keirby*)

Foreword

As Mayor of this great town of ours, I am delighted to write this foreword as an acknowledgement of a century of Wolverhampton.

We have a wealth of history which is well documented; notably, Wulfrunians have participated in two distinct millennium celebrations in recent years. The first, in 1985, acknowledged the granting of the Charter to Lady Wulfruna in AD 985 by the then King Ethelred. More recently in 1994 Wulfrunians celebrated the millennium of our wonderful St Peter's Church.

During this last century our population has been enriched with races and cultures from across the world. We have become truly cosmopolitan and are living and working together in harmony for the betterment of our entire community.

Our motto is 'Out of Darkness Cometh Light'. It has been in use since 1 May 1899, and might encourage a belief in improvement and enlightenment through learning and development over time; if so, then I am delighted to confirm that as the last Mayor this century we are making excellent progress towards the new era.

Like many industrial towns Wolverhampton has had its fair share of difficulties over this last century. Our town, which saw the birth of the traffic light, was home to the Sunbeam motor car and was heavily dependent on the steel and metal related industries, has witnessed unprecedented levels of unemployment throughout the 1970s and '80s. It is a testimony to the character of all of its citizens that we have emerged in the 1990s as a town re-energised and more determined than ever to succeed in enhancing the quality of life for all sections of our community. New relationships have been encouraged and new partnerships have been formed which will ensure a new strength of purpose as we go forward to face the new challenges that the new millennium will bring.

Our hotels, pubs, clubs and restaurants offer something for everyone. We have a busy university, excellent public services and good communications between Wolverhampton and our neighbouring towns: most recently we have seen the arrival of the Metro, which links Wolverhampton, Bilston, West Bromwich and Birmingham. Our night-time entertainment venues are thriving, with many thousands of visitors coming into our town to enjoy themselves. All in all, Wolverhampton is a great place to be.

As we approach the end of the era and the dawn of a new one I am conscious of the new partnerships which have been created which reinforce our commitment to a better Wolverhampton for all. I am very honoured to be Mayor at such an historic time, particularly as Wolverhampton may soon become a city. I look forward to the challenges with hope and optimism.

Councillor Peter Bilson, Mayor of Wolverhampton
1999/2000

George Dugmore established his cycle business on the Bilston Road in 1904, congratulating himself on his farsighted investment in a business that was rapidly expanding. A few years later he turned down the offer of a Ford dealership, believing that the motor car would be a nine day wonder! The picture was taken in 1912, when the family and their bicycles posed for Mr Bennett Clark, Wolverhampton's famous photographer. (*Ethel Wild's Collection*)

Britain: A Century of Change

Children gathered around an early wireless set in the 1920s. The speed
and forms of communication were to change dramatically as the century
advanced. (*Barnaby's Picture Library*)

The delirious rejoicing at the news of the Relief of Mafeking, during the Boer War in May 1900, is a colourful historical moment. But, in retrospect, the introduction that year of the first motor bus was rather more important, signalling another major adjustment to town life. In the previous 60 years railway stations, post-and-telegraph offices, police and fire stations, gas works and gasometers, new livestock markets and covered markets, schools, churches, football grounds, hospitals and asylums, water pumping stations and sewerage plants had totally altered the urban scene, as the country's population tripled and over 70 per cent were born in or moved to the towns.

When Queen Victoria died in 1901, she was measured for her coffin by her grandson Kaiser Wilhelm, the London prostitutes put on black mourning and the blinds came down in the villas and terraces spreading out from the old town centres. These centres were reachable by train and tram, by the new bicycles and still newer motor cars, con-nected by the new telephone, and lit by gas or even electricity. The shops may have been full of British-made cotton and woollen clothing but the grocers and butchers were selling cheap Danish bacon, Argentinian beef, Australasian mutton, tinned or dried fish and fruit from Canada, California and South Africa. Most of these goods were carried in British-built-and-crewed ships, burning Welsh steam coal.

As the first decade moved on, the Open Spaces Act meant more parks, bowling greens and cricket pitches. The first state pensions came in, together with higher taxation and death duties. These were raised mostly to pay for the new Dreadnought battleships needed to maintain naval superiority over Germany, and deter them from war. But the deterrent did not work. The First World War transformed the place of women, as they took over many men's jobs. Its other legacies were the war memorials which joined the statues of Victorian worthies in main squares round the land. After 1918 death duties bit even harder and a quarter of England changed hands in a few years.

Women working as porters on the Great Western Railway, Paddington, *c. 1917. (W.L. Kenning/ Adrian Vaughan Collection)*

The multiple shop – the chain store – appeared in the high street: Sainsburys, Maypole, Lipton's, Home & Colonial, the Fifty Shilling Tailor, Burton, Boots, W.H. Smith. The shopper was spoilt for choice, attracted by the brash fascias and advertising hoardings for national brands like Bovril, Pears Soap, and Ovaltine. Many new buildings began to be seen, such as garages, motor showrooms, picture palaces (cinemas), 'palais de dance', and the bow-windowed, pebble-dashed, tile-hung, half-timbered houses that were built as ribbon-development along the roads and new bypasses or on the new estates nudging the green belts.

During the 1920s cars became more reliable and sophisticated as well as commonplace, with developments like the electric self-starter making them easier for women to drive. Who wanted to turn a crank handle in the new short skirt? This was, indeed, the electric age as much as the motor era. Trolley buses, electric trams and trains extended mass transport and electric light replaced gas in the street and the home, which itself was groomed by the vacuum cleaner.

A major jolt to the march onward and upward was administered by the Great Depression of the early 1930s. The older British industries – textiles, shipbuilding, iron, steel, coal – were already under pressure from foreign competition when this worldwide slump arrived, cutting exports by half in two years and producing 3 million unemployed (and still rising) by 1932. Luckily there were new diversions to alleviate the misery. The 'talkies' arrived in the cinemas; more and more radios and gramophones were to be found in people's homes; there were new women's magazines, with fashion, cookery tips and problem pages; football pools; the flying feats of women pilots like Amy Johnson; the Loch Ness Monster; cheap chocolate and the drama of Edward VIII's abdication.

Father and child cycling past Buckingham Palace on VE Day, 8 May 1945. (Hulton Getty Picture Collection)

Things were looking up again by 1936 and unemployment was down to 2 million. New light industry was booming in the Home Counties as factories struggled to keep up with the demand for radios, radiograms, cars and electronic goods including the first television sets. The threat from Hitler's Germany meant rearmament, particularly of the airforce, which stimulated aircraft and aero engine firms. If you were lucky and lived in the south, there was good money to be earned. A semi-detached house cost £450, a Morris Cowley £150. People may have smoked like chimneys but life expectancy, since 1918, was up by 15 years while the birth rate had almost halved. The fifty-four hour week was down to forty-eight hours and there were 9 million radio licences by 1939.

In some ways it is the little memories that seem to linger longest from the Second World War: the kerbs painted white to show up in the blackout, the rattle of ack-ack shrapnel on roof tiles, sparrows killed

11

by bomb blast, painting your legs brown and then adding a black seam down the back to simulate stockings. The biggest damage, apart from London, was in the south-west (Plymouth, Bristol) and the Midlands (Coventry, Birmingham). Postwar reconstruction was rooted in the Beveridge Report which set out the expectations for the Welfare State. This, together with the nationalisation of the Bank of England, coal, gas, electricity and the railways, formed the programme of the Labour government in 1945. At this time the USA was calling in its debts and Britain was beggared by the war, yet still administering its Empire.

Times were hard in the late 1940s, with rationing even more stringent than during the war. Yet this was, as has been said, 'an innocent and well-behaved era'. The first let-up came in 1951 with the Festival of Britain and then there was another fillip in 1953 from the Coronation, which incidentally gave a huge boost to the spread of TV. By 1954 leisure

A family gathered around their television set in the 1950s. (*Hulton Getty Picture Collection*)

motoring had been resumed but the Comet – Britain's best hope for taking on the American aviation industry – suffered a series of mysterious crashes. The Suez debacle of 1956 was followed by an acceleration in the withdrawal from Empire, which had begun in 1947 with the Independence of India. Consumerism was truly born with the advent of commercial TV and most homes soon boasted washing machines, fridges, electric irons and fires.

The *Lady Chatterley* obscenity trial in 1960 was something of a straw in the wind for what was to follow in that decade. A collective loss of inhibition seemed to sweep the land, as stately home owners opened up, the Beatles and the Rolling Stones transformed popular music, and retailing, cinema and the theatre were revolutionised. Designers, hairdressers, photographers and models moved into places vacated by an Establishment put to flight by the new breed of satirists spawned by *Beyond the Fringe* and *Private Eye*.

In the 1970s Britain seems to have suffered a prolonged hangover after the excesses of the previous decade. Ulster, inflation and union troubles were not made up for by entry into the EEC, North Sea Oil, Women's Lib or, indeed, Punk Rock. Mrs Thatcher applied the corrective in the 1980s, as the country moved more and more from its old manufacturing base over to providing services, consulting, advertising, and expertise in the 'invisible' market of high finance or in IT. Britain entertained the world with *Cats*, *Phantom of the Opera*, *Four Weddings and a Funeral*, *The Full Monty*, *Mr Bean* and the *Teletubbies*.

The post-1945 townscape has seen changes to match those in the worlds of work, entertainment and politics. In 1956 the Clean Air Act served notice on smogs and pea-souper fogs, smuts and blackened buildings, forcing people to stop burning coal and go over to smokeless sources of heat and energy. In the same decade some of the best urban building took place in the 'new towns' like Basildon, Crawley, Stevenage and Harlow. Elsewhere open warfare was declared on slums and what was labelled inadequate, cramped, back-to-back, two-up, two-down, housing. The new 'machine for living in' was a flat in a high-rise block. The architects and planners who promoted these were in league with the traffic engineers, determined to keep the motor car moving

Carnaby Street in the 1960s. (*Barnaby's Picture Library*)

The Millennium Dome at Greenwich, 1999. (*Michael Durnan/Barnaby's Picture Library*)

whatever the price in multi-storey car parks, meters, traffic wardens and ring roads.

The old pollutant, coal smoke, was replaced by petrol and diesel exhaust, and traffic noise. Even in the back garden it was hard to find peace as motor mowers, then leaf blowers and strimmers made themselves heard, and the neighbours let you share their choice of music from their powerful new amplifiers, whether you wanted to or not. Fast food was no longer only a pork pie in a pub or fish-and-chips. There were Indian curry houses, Chinese take-aways and American-style hamburgers, while the drinker could get away from beer in a wine bar. Under the impact of television the big Gaumonts and Odeons closed or were rebuilt as multi-screen cinemas, while the palais de dance gave way to discos and clubs.

From the late 1960s the introduction of listed buildings and conservation areas, together with the growth of preservation societies, put a brake on 'comprehensive redevelopment'. Now the new risk at the end of the 1990s is that town centres may die, as shoppers are attracted to the edge-of-town supermarkets surrounded by parking space, where much more than food and groceries can be bought. The ease of the one-stop shop represents the latest challenge to the good health of our towns. But with care, ingenuity and a determination to keep control of our environment, this challenge can be met.

Wolverhampton: An Introduction

Wolverhampton in the twentieth century has striven to cultivate a separate identity to that of its neighbours – it is neither part of rural South Staffordshire, nor is it part of the industrialised Black Country. Its development is inextricably interwoven with both but it has wished to be its own place – a town enjoying proximity to both worlds and delighting in being a 'frontier'.

It began the twentieth century with a flamboyant display of self-confidence – the Arts & Industry Exhibition of 1902 – and it ended the century with another display of assertiveness in which it applied to be given the status of a city. In between it has had its ups and downs, its moments of glory and its times of identity crisis and self-doubt. In 1968 its MP, Enoch Powell, expressed doubt as to whether future Wulfrunians could live in harmony in his famous 'Rivers of Blood' speech. He told a story of a white Wulfrunian intimidated by newcomers. The example he

A sign of the times. The 2nd Wolverhampton Scouts (St Luke's) line up for a photograph, but it's 1916 and the war is on so we find one young man in soldier's uniform, and another in what appears to be RFC uniform. They were photographed at the vicarage on Goldthorn Hill. (*Phil Bennet Collection*)

quoted was never found but his speech labelled the town as some kind of xenophobic backwater – an image from which it took some time to recover.

Ironically, Wolverhampton has always owed much to 'incomers'. In the nineteenth century it grew and prospered because people came to work here. By the beginning of the twentieth century it was a town of about 90,000 people – the largest town in Staffordshire, and one with a long and distinguished history stretching back to Anglo-Saxon times. There could be no denying that this population growth was the result of its proximity to the South Staffordshire Coalfield and the development of the iron trades.

When Queen Victoria came to Wolverhampton in 1866 she arrived by train and took a horse-drawn carriage through an arch of coal; when visitors arrived at the town's 1902 Exhibition they journeyed down to West Park in a brand-new electric tram to find iron gates which demonstrated that metal bashing could be a symbol of both industry and art. The visitor today can arrive on the brand-new Metro, fighting with motor traffic, ring roads and traffic lights to get here, to be greeted by nightclubs, shopping complexes and a town, or maybe a city, with a bewildering diversity of architecture and a delightful mixture of cultures.

A Sense of Occasion. Residents of Winchester Road, Fordhouses, line up for a photograph on VE Day, 1945. The war is coming to an end (see page 82). (*Jack Endean*)

This book tries to take in all these changes and to tour the town era by era, looking at buildings, events, transport, work, leisure and people.

Local coalmasters and ironmasters seemed pretty gloomy in the early years of this century, but manufacturers found that their engineering skills were capable of producing goods that were in demand ranging from cycles, motor-cycles and cars to electrical equipment, holloware and enamelled goods, and varnishes. Much of the town centre was very new and additions such as the Library, the Wholesale Market, and Hospital buildings were still being made. Wolverhampton was cultivating its Edwardian suburbs, and experimenting with 'Garden City' concepts at Parkdale and Fallings Park. The first municipal houses were built and people realised that nineteenth-century slums would have to be cleared. Public transport had been municipalised, as was the supply of electricity, gas and water.

Wulfrunians could enjoy everything from nights at the opera to flying shows in Edwardian times, but that era came to an end in August 1914. The 6th Battalion of the Staffordshire Regiment marched off to war in October of that year, and, like all sections of the armed forces, suffered terrible casualties. The irony is that manufacturing

A Sense of History. PC O'Connor and a trainee stand by the Roll of Honour in Bilston Street Police Station. The West Midlands Police replaced the Borough force in 1966; the Police Station opened in 1992. The Roll of Honour lists officers who died in three twentieth-century conflicts, the South African War, and the two world wars. The three plaques commemorate three Wolverhampton policemen who have died locally during the course of duty. (*West Midlands Police*)

towns can be busy and prosperous as a result of war, although the cost may be loss of life, dislocation and a moratorium on work that might improve the fabric and health of the town.

The inter-war years encompassed a variety of experiences for Wulfrunians – a non-stop variety show of 'Good News – Bad News'. A good example of this was found in the world of motor vehicle manufacture: at one minute it seemed that the town would be the capital of the country's automotive industry, the next minute well-known manufacturers were wiped out by slumps. New manufacturers were welcomed to the town – notably Courtaulds, Goodyear and Boulton Paul Aircraft. Wolverhampton greatly expanded during the inter-war years by absorbing neighbouring territory (Heath Town UDC and part of Seisdon RDC, for example), and by building vast tracts of municipal and private suburbia. In the town centre architectural 'modernism' arrived in various forms, and Edwardian concepts like the electric tram were eventually consigned to extinction – for the time being!

Like other industrial centres that were used to ups and downs, Wolverhampton experienced a more steady sense of being on the up in the years that led into the Second World War. From 1939 onwards Wolverhampton was working round the clock: it was a very busy place indeed, although this is something that is very difficult to show in photographs. What is more plainly visible in photographs is the relief that it is all over in the pictures taken of VE Day parties.

Although there were great social changes going on in the immediate postwar years, ranging from the introduction of the Welfare State to the invention of the Teenager, the architectural environment changed little. The 'look' of Wolverhampton really changes dramatically in the 1960s with a full assault on many treasures in the town centre. It probably took the 1970s to complete the work of the 1960s – even then the Ring Road was not completed until the middle of the next decade. Photography has been used self-consciously to record such changes, because in recent times people have realised that photographs make historical statements.

Modern times have been more challenging to record – how do you describe the ups, downs and up-agains of a town's morale in photographs? You will notice that people feature in this section more than the built environment: that is because people have been at the centre of the noteworthy changes, upheavals, and moments of progress, of the last two decades. Perhaps the time has come for Wolverhampton to put on a major exhibition in West Park in 2002 – with an extension of the Metro laid down to the gates! We will be able to show the world how it took 900 years for Wolverhampton to become the town we see at the beginning of this book, and 100 years to recover, while we are now ready to march into the new Millennium!

The Start of the Century

G.H. Bradford's Christmas card of 1900. Mr Bradford, who appears on his own card, was Sales Manager at the Star Cycle Company. At the end of the nineteenth century Wolverhampton had become a centre of the cycle industry. Out of this a motor car and motor-cycle industry was about to emerge. (*The late Bert Bradford*)

Wolverhampton began and ended the twentieth century waiting for the electric trams to start running! The trams entered service between the town centre and Newhampton Road East on 1 May 1902 – the same day that Wolverhampton's great Industrial & Arts Exhibition opened in West Park. (Note the car on the left carries an 'Exhibition' destination board while standing in the brand-new depot built in Cleveland Road.) (*Millennium Collection*)

The Great Exhibition of 1902 was an attempt to promote Wolverhampton and to celebrate the town's progress at the beginning of the twentieth century. Visitors could travel to the show, in West Park, by electric tram and then entered the exhibition via these gates, built locally by Bayliss Jones and Bayliss. BJB had been in business since the 1830s and were well-known manufacturers of ornamental wrought-iron work. The Exhibition Hall seen behind the gates was demolished after the event. (*Author's Collection*)

In the early 1900s Wolverhampton made a major contribution to replacing the horse with new technology. Even so, local businessmen still owned a horse and trap as a sign of wealth. William Farnell was in the leather trade, with a shop in Snow Hill and a tannery in Walsall. He is seen here taking his wife, Fanny, and his sons, Jack and Frank, for a Sunday afternoon jaunt from their home in Waterloo Road down to West Park. (*Barbara Farnell*)

George Bradford, seen here with his wife Louise and son Albert, was more 'progressive' and by 1909 travelled in a Briton two-cylinder motor car. Edward Lisle Jnr had just started production of Briton cars in the Stewart Street factory used by the Star Cycle Co. Note the wooden wheels, acetylene headlamps, absence of windscreen and round petrol tank behind the seat. (*The late Bert Bradford*)

21

Wolverhampton's cycle industry of the 1900s was based in an industrial quarter of the town stretching from Blakenhall to Graisley. Here is the cycle building and assembly department at Rudge & Wedge's works in Pelham Street at the turn of the century. Note the absence of artificial lighting and the fact that workers felt compelled to wear hats. (*Author's Collection*)

The public face of Wolverhampton's cycle industry was presented at trade fairs in elaborate displays like this one. George Bradford of the Star Cycle Co. is seen on the left, while the man with a notebook is Vic Calcutt, the Sales Manager. George's heart was in motoring rather than cycling, and Vic had the misfortune to be run over by an electric tram in Penn Fields. (*The late Bert Bradford*)

A town-centre view in the 1900s looks down North Street towards the town's Victorian town hall. On the right is Tom B. Dobson's Staffordshire Seed Store and the front of the Empire Saloon. The latter formed a flank of the frontage of the Empire Theatre – a variety theatre that had opened at the end of 1898. It introduced twice-nightly shows in 1900 and spent the decade in fierce competition with a rival variety theatre in Bilston Street. (*Ken Rock Collection*)

Out in the suburbs in the 1900s. This view of the Newhampton Road looks towards the town's western suburb of Whitmore Reans in which a great many Edwardian homes were built in the 1900s. The 1902 Education Act propelled Wolverhampton into extending its secondary educational provision. The Higher Grade School seen here was opened in 1894 and the 'Higher' section of this school was granted 'secondary' status as a response to the 1902 Act – hoping to retain pupils until they matriculated at fifteen. (*Ken Rock Collection*)

Out in the suburbs again, 1900s. Edwardian Wolverhampton began to extend south-westwards along the Penn Road as seen here. Its proximity to the town centre is underlined by the sight of St Peter's Church in the distance, although this impression has now been swept aside by the widening of Penn Road and the construction of the Ring Road. On the left is the junction with Lea Road with Mander Street in the distance. Behind the fence on the right is The Hollies. (*Ken Rock Collection*)

The junction with Mander Street can be seen on the left in this view of the other side of Penn Road as it entered the Edwardian town centre. Sydney Street and Ablow Street on the right will give you your bearings, but St Paul's Church and the buildings on the right have entirely disappeared. This is a later view than the one above as the electric tram tracks have now been extended towards the Penn Road. Behind the cameraman they turned into Lea Road and made for Penn Fields – commencing operation in 1909. (*Ken Rock Collection*)

Exactly one mile's walk from the location shown opposite was Wolverhampton's High Level station. Services from this station commenced in 1852, and the architecture is the work of local man Edward Banks. As seen here in the 1900s, the frontage welcomes passengers to the services of the London & North Western Rly, the Midland Rly and the Great Western Rly, the latter reached at 'Low Level' via a subway. The horse-drawn carriages were another local product – built by the Forder Co. of Cleveland Road. (*Millennium Collection*)

Lichfield Street had been pushed through from Queen Square to Victoria Square in the 1880s. By the 1900s it was fully developed and in 1902 the trams began running along Lichfield Street on their way to the Great Exhibition. Note the absence of any overhead wiring as a result of Wolverhampton's controversial decision to use the Lorain surface contact form of electrification. The scale of the buildings reflected Wolverhampton's sense of its importance, and the Art Gallery, on the left, was evidence of public benefaction and civic pride. (*Millennium Collection*)

Trams commenced running from Victoria Square (for the railway station) out along the Waterloo Road and Stafford Road to Bushbury in August 1904, serving suburbs developing on the northern side of the town. At the Bushbury Lane terminus Driver Vaughan waits to take his tramcar back to the town centre. Car no. 3 was one of three cars built by the Electric Railway & Tramway Carriage Co., supplied in 1902. (*Andrew Vaughan*)

It is now difficult to imagine that the tram terminus at the junction of Bushbury Lane with the Stafford Road was once on the outskirts of town. New Edwardian housing extends up the left-hand side of Stafford Road and a car can be seen heading for the countryside. This location is now a crowded dual carriageway, part of the A449's passage through Wolverhampton. (*Ken Rock Collection*)

A still moment in an Edwardian summer is captured in this view of the junction of Wadham's Hill and Waterloo Road, in a 'Pipers' series postcard. The elegant Victorian mansion in the background was the home of the Kidson family. Today this view has been obliterated by the construction of the Ring Road and Tarmac House. (*Ken Rock Collection*)

In the 1900s an ambitious Garden Suburb was planned in Fallings Park, just off the Cannock Road. Co-ownership and a well-planned environment formed the background to this scheme in which good quality housing would be within the economic reach of the better-paid artisan. These cottages in Victoria Road were designed by local architect W.J. Oliver and were 'opened' on 26 February 1908 by the Bishop of Lichfield. The scheme's development was halted by the First World War, but these houses still stand. (*Ken Rock Collection*)

The vanguard of Wolverhampton's working-class population were the skilled engineers – machinists, rather than the metal bashers who beavered away during the previous century. This turn-of-the-century view of the belt-driven machine shop at the Star Cycle Co. in Stewart Street produced all the components needed for the firm's products. Even when Wolverhampton's industries ceased to make the finished product, the town continued the tradition of component manufacture. (*Author's Collection*)

The Electric Construction Company built a huge factory close to the Stafford Road in the 1890s to produce heavy electrical machinery – an example of Wolverhampton's move into the 'new' industries of that time. This was the 'small' erecting shop, lined with machinery belt-driven from a single shaft, and illuminated with electric light – as might be expected in such a company. In the 1900s the company supplied electric motors and generating equipment to customers all over the world. (*Author's Collection*)

The production of enamel signs brought together two strands of Wolverhampton's industrial traditions. The nineteenth-century metal-bashing tradition created local firms that rolled out sheets of iron while the tradition of japanning and enamelling made us experts in decorating such surfaces. The 1900s saw unprecedented demand for enamelled signs and adverts. Work proceeds in front of the furnaces in the fusing and enamelling department at the Elgin Works of Orme Evans & Co. (*Author's Collection*)

One of Wolverhampton's most famous producers of enamel signs was the Chromographic Enamel Co. on the Dudley Road. Examples of their work are often found on preserved railway stations today. This picture shows the no. 1 Brushing Shop and seems to have been posed to show the finished products, the boss and his workforce. (*Author's Collection*)

29

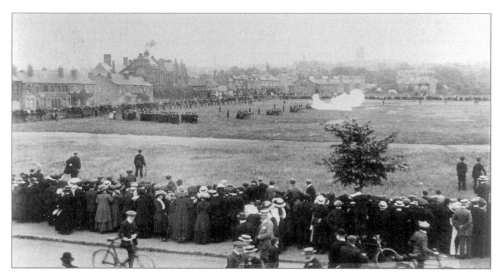

To mark the Coronation of King George V the Royal Salute is fired from the field between Newhampton Road and West Park, 22 June 1911. This view from Devon Road looks past the Higher Grade School (see page 27) towards the centre of town. The field had been used at the time of the 1902 Exhibition, was sometimes used for pasture and hay-making, and part of it was eventually used as a sports field for the school. (*Ken Rock Collection*)

To provide adequate secondary education for girls to matriculation standard the local Education Committee had to build the Girls High School just off the Tettenhall Road. The school opened in 1911 and this picture shows the girls cultivating the newly created gardens in the school's pastoral surroundings. Obviously the curriculum was not entirely academic. (*Ken Rock Collection*)

Entertainment in the 1900s: A 'Pierrot' show takes the open-air stage at Newbridge one summer in the early 1900s. The artistes are believed to be 'Battersby's Pierrots' – Harry Battersby had run theatres in Bilston and Wednesbury in the past, and presumably ran the pierrots to keep in touch with the business. A trip out to Newbridge or Tettenhall on the electric tram was a popular leisure-time excursion. (*Ken Rock Collection*)

From 1 January 1910 the Kinematograph Act came into force and there was a race to see who could open Wolverhampton's first licensed cinema. The Electric Theatre in Queen Square beat all competitors and opened at the end of that month – next door to the Staffordshire Bank, which by then had become the National Provincial. Just one car is to be seen among the trams and pedestrians. Note the town's fire escape always kept by Albert's statue, and the former horse tram terminus. (*Ken Rock Collection*)

There was an explosion in leisure and entertainment provision in the 1900s. Pat Collins' travelling funfair had been coming to the Market Patch between St Peter's Church and North Street three times a year since the 1890s and in this picture is seen presenting all the latest Edwardian fairground tackle – the gallopers, a switchback scenic railway (on the left), the steam yachts and 'Razzle Dazzle' (on the right). (*Alex Chatwin Collection*)

In about 1907 a roller-skating craze swept Britain and every town worth mentioning had to have a rink. Large sheds clad in sheets of corrugated iron sprang up, like this one at Short Heath, and with a live band and suitable decorations was able to provide an exciting environment in which to skate. The craze did not endure with sufficient support to maintain the viability of such halls, and most were put to other uses. (*Ken Rock Collection*)

Alongside the expanding worlds of entertainment and leisure, the 1900s also witnessed developments in the sporting world. Wolverhampton Wanderers Football Club had been at the Molineux since 1889. After a shaky start to the twentieth century they joined the Second Division in 1906, and beat Newcastle 3–1 in the 1908 Cup Final. The match was recorded on film and postcards like this one, in the 'Wulfruna' series, went on sale. (*Ken Rock Collection*)

Meanwhile gentlemen out in the suburbs had formed the Penn Fields Hockey Team and this card, in the 'Avon' series, was printed to preserve their identities for posterity. The team was led by F.H. Whitehouse, a Wolverhampton solicitor, and their ground was in Coalway Lane. (*Ken Rock Collection*)

Building the canal system had facilitated the nineteenth-century industrialisation of Wolverhampton, and made a lasting contribution to the landscape. This 1900s 'Pipers' postcard view seems to show people out walking the towpath, and the Shropshire Union Canal Co. narrow-boat *Belvide* pausing by the bank. Wolverhampton's gas works forms the backdrop; it was served by a canal arm on the right. The abutment of the bridge carrying the railway sidings into the gas works can still be seen – close to Wolverhampton's 'Science Park' of the 1990s. (*Ken Rock Collection*)

A much more twentieth-century mode of transport was flying. Wolverhampton played its part in early flying ventures and has since been much preoccupied by the aerospace industry. C. Grahame White was a relatively unknown aviator as he flew over Wolverhampton in 1910 – having brought his plane to the Dunstall Park Aviation Meeting by train! (He went on to greater things, including founding Hendon Aerodrome.) A certain amount of licence has been taken in this picture as the plane did not stray far from Dunstall during its hour-and-a-half flight. (*Ken Rock Collection*)

Despite the local interest in promoting motorised transport, many Edwardian businesses in Wolverhampton still relied on the horse. Mr Smart ran the West End Fondant at 40a Bath Road, Chapel Ash. It was therefore a simple matter to pose his transport by the South Gate entrance to West Park in about 1910. (*Mrs Booth*)

Harry Hespley was a driver/roundsman for the Wolverhampton & District Co-operative Society, who had been baking their own bread in Blakenhall since 1902. The turn-out of the horse with its plaited mane suggests that it may have just taken part in one of the Society's annual parades. The picture was taken in about 1912. (*Reg Hespley*)

In about 1912 the 2nd Wolverhampton Baden Powell Scouts, based at St Luke's Church, Blakenhall, pose for the photographer in the garden of the vicarage on Goldthorn Hill. (*Phil Bennett Collection*)

The Springfield Brewery Fire Brigade pose for the photographer inside Butler's Brewery, on their horse-drawn appliance, *c.* 1912. Left to right: T. Price, J. Willis, H. Birch, H. Turner, Mr Cooper, T. Ambrose, G. Shelley, T. Appleby and R. Rendison. The picture was rediscovered in 1946 and was reproduced in Butler's magazine. (*John Spittle Collection*)

The Wolverhampton Police in about 1900, at a time when it was led by Captain Lindsay Burnett, a military man with a 'despotic' style, according to the contemporary press. This may be why he, and his deputy, appear to be wearing Yeomanry-style jackets. (*West Midlands Police*)

The Wolverhampton Borough Engineer, George Green, his Deputy, W.S. Russell, and members of his staff pose for the camera in front of the conservatory in West Park in 1903. On the right is Silvanus Bennett (Works Foreman), who was killed in October 1917 in an accident at the town's baths (see page 2). (*Phil Bennett Collection*)

In 1913 William Perry & Co. started building the new railway from Wolverhampton to Wombourne – a scheme that had started life as a plan to link Wolverhampton to Bridgnorth. Its construction was delayed and its 1925 opening makes it one of the last passenger-carrying lines to open in Britain. Its construction used the contractor's locomotives, horsepower, and mechanical excavators to dig out cuttings at Castlecroft. (*the late Billy Day Collection*)

At Oxley Junction, just north of Aldersley, a new viaduct had to be built over the Staffordshire & Worcestershire Canal in 1913 to carry the new line to Wombourne. The contractor first built a temporary bridge across the canal to carry his own light railway, and this can be seen in the foreground. After the closure and lifting of the line in the 1960s the trackbed south of this point became a linear park and public footpath. (*Ernest Milner*)

The First World War

'Richy' Richardson, of Dunkley Street, stands on the left in the uniform that he wore during the Boer War. He served in the Army again during the First World War and then worked for Phillips & Jones, the Wolverhampton furnishers. He managed their town centre shop during the 1930s. Listed as a reservist, he was called up again in 1939 and served briefly in the Second World War. One wonders how many Wulfrunians served in three conflicts. (*Anne Richardson*)

Above: Zedekiah Green walked from Wolverhampton to Newport, South Wales, in 1914 in search of work, joined the Army when the war started and sent a telegram home to his family to tell them the news. Three years later the War Office wrote to Mrs Green to say that Zedekiah had died from dysentery and malaria in Salonika. (*Marion Winspur Collection*)

Right: Private Reg Caswell, in the Royal Army Ordnance Corps, *c.* 1917. His father, T.R. Caswell, ran clothes shops at 62 Dudley Street and 13 Queen Square. The latter appears on many postcard views of Queen Square – like the one on page 56. (*Phil Bennett Collection*)

On 5 October 1914 a Civic Farewell was given to the 6th Battalion South Staffordshire Regiment as it left for the war. This Bennett Clark picture turned into a postcard shows the new gardens (opened in June 1907) at the base of St Peter's Church and the Wholesale Market. Note the crowds and the presence of the Scout band. Many Wulfrunians served in the local battalion of the South Staffords during both world wars. (*Ken Rock Collection*)

Denis James Fallon spent his boyhood at 119 Villiers Street and then volunteered to join the Army during the First World War – possibly lying about his age! He fought at the Somme in 1916 and was one of the few in his regiment to survive the battle. He saw the war out in Italy – near Lake Garda – and then returned to Wolverhampton to become a foreman for Charles Hayward. He lived to the age of 83. He is seen here with his sisters, Norah and Gertie. (*Anne Richardson*)

Many Wulfrunians did not return from the First World War and are named on the War Memorial in St Peter's Gardens. No memorial was erected to the two VCs associated with the town but Seaman D.M. Harris is commemorated in St Peter's Gardens. Douglas Morris Harris was a heroic wireless operator who continued to man his post on board his shell-torn ship, the drifter *Floandi*, until killed by enemy gunfire. He died on 15 May 1917. (*Ned Williams*)

On the Home Front, women were taken on to replace men who had gone to war, and to help industry move into wartime production. Women are seen here in the works canteen at Chubb's factory on the Wednesfield Road. (*Ken Rock Collection*)

The Sunbeam Motor Car Co. in Villiers Street continued to produce cars after the war started – mainly for use as military staff cars, as well as chassis for ambulances. A shortage of aero engines led to the Ministry of Munitions directing Sunbeam to concentrate all their efforts on production of aero engines – as seen here. (*Millennium Collection*)

The Star Engineering Co. produced these 50 cwt trucks in the Frederick Street factory for the British and Russian governments, and this posed postcard view describes itself as 'somewhere on the front'. (*David Evans*)

This postcard was produced to promote the Star Mobile Marconi Transmitting Station, which after inspection by King Alfonso was supplied to the Spanish War Office and then to other European customers. King Alfonso's inspection is depicted in the scenes on the card. (*David Evans*)

43

The Great Western Railway's staff ambulance class at Oxley in 1914 faced the prospect of using their first aid skills during a time of war. The locomotive is 4050, 'Princess Alice', a 4–6–0 of the Star class, introduced in 1906. (*Ken Rock Collection*)

The Drill Hall in Devon Road, close to West Park, provided space to practise gun drill – but not quite under the conditions that might prevail on the Western Front. (*Wolverhampton Archives*)

The Inter-war Years

The Wolverhampton Co-operative Society began acquiring premises in Lichfield Street during the war. When the war was over these were gradually integrated into a parade of shops which began with the Cosy Café, opened in 1921. In this picture Harry Hespley poses with the café staff. Postwar hemlines are beginning to rise. (*Reg Hespley*)

Wolverhampton's tramways had survived with a minimum of maintenance and investment during the war. After the war, renewal was urgent, and conversion to conventional overhead current supply seemed necessary. Pole planting began at the beginning of 1921, and had reached the Penn Fields end of Lea Road by the October of that year. Car 61 is seen here on trials of the new system in Lea Road, hence the incorrect route number. (*Millennium Collection*)

The trams dominate the street scenes of the immediate postwar years, but by 1923 the conversion of routes to trackless trolleybuses had begun. Lea Road, seen here in the mid-1920s, lost its tram service on 20 March 1927. A temporary bus service then ran until the trolleybuses began running down Lea Road on 11 July. (*Ken Rock Collection*)

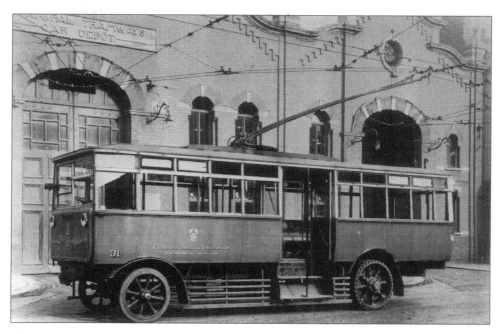

The first generation of Wolverhampton trolleybuses were single-deckers, first introduced on the service to Wednesfield in 1923. No. 31 – a Tillings Stevens, Dobson-bodied, 3-seater is seen here in 1927, standing outside the Cleveland Road Depot. They looked very smart in their apple green and primrose yellow livery, introduced in 1923, but note that passengers had to endure a ride on solid tyres. (*Millennium Collection*)

Wolverhampton was proud of its role as a trolleybus pioneer and the record expansion of its network of services. The two Wolverhampton commercial vehicle builders, Sunbeam and Guy, also became known internationally for trolleybus production. In this view, taken in about 1929, Guy six-wheel trolleybuses pose outside the Cleveland Road Depot. (*Millennium Collection*)

Wolverhampton Corporation's motor bus no. 47 was the first six-wheeler in the country. It was built by Guy Motors, with a Dobson open rear staircase body, in 1926. It is parked outside the Town Hall in North Street. The bus is so new that it carries no destination box. The party may be about to take the bus down to the Floral Fete, held in July in West Park, or explore the new routes out to Wolverhampton's extended suburbs. (*Millennium Collection*)

Wolverhampton also acquired fame with its pioneering introduction of traffic lights in Princes Square towards the end of the 1920s – at first using a temporary four-faced set of lights manually operated by a policeman. This picture was taken in August 1929, before the lights were rebuilt on a more permanent basis. (*Jan Endean Collection*)

In the 1920s pedestrians still filled the streets of Wolverhampton on public occasions. In January 1925 crowds had turned out to witness the funeral of PC Willetts, a young constable murdered in Vicarage Road. On 22 July of the same year crowds can be seen here at the funeral of Fireman David Southwick, who had served the town for twenty-one years. Note the Police Band on the left. (*F.J. Jennings*)

David Webster was Wolverhampton's first civilian Chief Constable, appointed in 1916. When he died in 1929 crowds turned out for a huge funeral, seen here passing from Queen Square into North Street. (*West Midlands Police*)

WOLVERHAMPTON WANDERERS

Front Row (Left to Right):—DAVISON, HARRINGTON, McMILLAN, BOWEN

Middle Row:—C. JOBEY, C. HOLLEY, LEGGE, TIMMINS, CADDICK, GEORGE

Back Row:—J. S. BAKER, A. H. HOSKINS, E. BARK

FOOTBALL CLUB, 1923-4.

AZACKERLEY, GETGOOD, PHILLIPSON, LEES, EDWARDS, SHAW.

AY, WATSON, J. DAVIS, A. H. OAKLEY, MAJOR A. HOLLOWAY.

T. W. SIMPSON, F. T. HOLLINS, H. MILLS.

An Arcade Studios postcard of the Wolves Team of 1923/24. (*Ken Rock Collection*)

Carnivals in the inter-war years were often held to raise funds for local hospitals, and could be guaranteed to fill the streets. On 29 June 1929 the Wolverhampton Hospitals Carnival was held. In this picture we can see the winning float – entered by Butlers Brewery. (*John Spittle Collection*)

At Whitsun 1925 Pat Collins was photographed on his fair held on the Market Patch. He is demonstrating a steering game on one of the side stalls. These were popular well-attended fairs, but just before the Second World War they were moved down to the Brickkiln Street Patch. Sixty-six-year-old Pat's personal presence on the ground was possibly prompted by his retirement as Walsall's MP. (*John Ray Collection*)

In the inter-war years Wolverhampton's streets were enlivened by some bright vehicle liveries adopted by local firms. This 1935 Morris Commercial van supplied to James Beattie Ltd with a body built by W.J. Smith of West Bromwich was in a bright green and cream livery. (*Jim Boulton Collection*)

The Morris Commercial van with a Smith body supplied to Wolverhampton Steam Laundry of Sweetman Street, Whitmore Reans, was in bright red, black and white. The firm built up a large fleet of vehicles to deal with increased demand for both commercial and domestic laundry work. (*Jim Boulton Collection*)

The Wolverhampton Steam Laundry employed a large female workforce at the laundry itself – occupying a large area between Sweetman Street and the Newhampton Road, Whitmore Reans. An unidentified worker is seen here by the Hydro in 1929. (*Les Clough, WSL*)

A Christmas Social held in the canteen at the Wolverhampton Steam Laundry, 1929. About half the firm's staff are seen here, including Major Carr, the firm's founder and his partner Mr Brocklebank, and their sons. The girls from the laundry outnumber the lads from the van-driving department, but the firm was very much one big happy family, and the floor was polished for weeks to be ready for this event. (*Les Clough*)

One of the Wolverhampton Steam Laundry's competitors, a shop belonging to the Express Valet Service, can be seen here at Penn Fields on a quiet summer afternoon in the 1930s. Trolleybus wires run overhead but there is a general absence of traffic. This and the one below are from the 'Piper' series of postcards. (*Ken Rock Collection*)

All seems quiet on the Penn Road, by Penn Post Office. Wolverhampton pushed its boundaries out along the Penn Road in 1934 in an area that had been part of the Rural District of Seisdon. The road is narrow enough to suspend both sets of trolleybus wires from a single pole. Could anyone imagine that this road would become a busy dual carriageway a few decades later? The van belonged to W.D. Warren – a butcher from Exchange Street. (*Ken Rock Collection*)

The town centre between the wars: Laurel & Hardy's *Bohemian Girl* is showing at the Queens Picture House during mid-June 1936 and traffic seems light. Note Caswell's shop at 13 Queen Square in the *Staffordshire Advertiser* Building (see page 40). (*Ken Rock Collection*)

A single-decker trolleybus passes the Hippodrome on its way into Queen Square. The Empire became the Hippodrome in February 1921 and remained a live variety theatre until a fire in 1956, apart from twelve months' use as a cinema from 1931 to 1932. (*Ken Rock Collection*)

Looking towards Queen Square from the top of Darlington Street in the 1920s. James Beattie was acquiring premises in Darlington Street in order to begin a major rebuild of the store in the 1930s, following the widening of Victoria Street. (*Ken Rock Collection*)

Lipton's shop on the corner of Queen Square and Exchange Street. Thomas Lipton began business in Scotland in the 1870s selling imported meat. In 1889 he diversified into groceries and tea, which he sold very cheaply. By the turn of the century Liptons were a fast growing 'multiple', always good at promotions such as the 'Bake a Cake' competition announced in the left-hand window. During rebuilding the premises in 1987 the Lipton name boards were exposed again for a short time. (*Shop in the Black Country Collection*)

By the 1930s stainless steel lettering on a black 'Vitrolite' fascia was the last word in shop exterior design. (The sills and blind fittings are also in stainless steel.) Shops such as milliners, dress shops, and interior decor shops like this one in Skinner Street also favoured an 'arcaded' frontage that maximised window display space. (*Shop in the Black Country Collection*)

Fenwick's in Pitt Street ventured into radio sets between the wars, a development that often grew out of the cycle business. They also ventured into fishing tackle and toys. (*Shop in the Black Country Collection*)

The view from Dudley Street towards Snow Hill was transformed in the inter-war years by the demolition of the Agricultural Hall in 1931 and its replacement with the Gaumont Palace Cinema. The latter opened on 5 September 1932 and ushered in the decade of 'super-cinema' building in fine style. On the extreme right is one of Wolverhampton's vanished pubs: the Swan & Peacock. (*Ken Rock Collection*)

Following in the footsteps of the Gaumont, other modern super-cinemas were built in the town centre and suburbs during the 1930s. Here, in Skinner Street, the Odeon is seen under construction on 3 June 1937. It was opened on 11 September 1937. It closed on 4 July 1983 and is now a banqueting suite with a fabulously decorated interior. (*Cyril Parker*)

The Dunstall Cinema, on Stafford Road, was very much the result of local initiative and investment. It opened on a very foggy 19 November 1934. It enjoyed barely two years of independence before being absorbed by the Odeon circuit, and lasted just under twenty-six years in total – closing on 5 November 1960. No sign of the cinema now exists. (*Ken Rock Collection*)

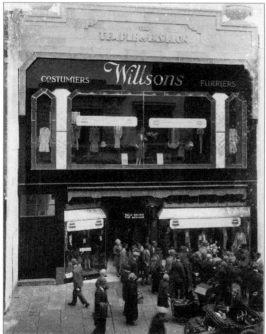

Two faces of modernity: Willson's shop in Dudley Street had a very modern frontage in the 1920s, using stainless steel lettering on Vitrolite (left), but even this had to be replaced in 1937 by the new frontage seen on the right. The frontage was treated in faience earthenware tiles (much favoured by cinemas!) and lettering which incorporated neon strip lighting. (*Shop in the Black Country Collection*)

Building the new Wolverhampton & South Staffordshire Technical College in Stafford Street in 1924 was hidden behind some nice 'period' advertising hoardings including classic Harold Lloyd and Tom Mix silent movies. The first section of the college, the Engineering Block, was opened in May 1926 by Princess Mary. Almost immediately it was decided to proceed with the extension that would take the college round into Wulfruna Street. (*University Collection*)

The Wulfruna Street section of the Technical College had its foundation stone laid on 17 October 1931 by Prince George, and was opened on 30 June 1933 by Marquess Dufferin, standing in for Lord Irwin, the President of the Board of Education. It was designed by Col. Lowbridge, architect to Staffordshire Education Committee. Students attending immediately superseded the number for which it had been planned! (*Ned Williams*)

Wolverhampton had several concert venues in the nineteenth century. By the 1920s it was suggested that we needed a twentieth-century version of the same facility. Eventually a fine modern Civic Hall was built next to the nineteenth-century Town Hall in North Street. Designed by E.D. Lyons and L. Israel of Ilford, it was opened in May 1938 with a Civic Ball featuring Jack Hylton and his Band. (*Ken Rock Collection*)

Wolverhampton's industries, and domestic grates, consumed vast quantities of coal in the inter-war years. Coal merchants flourished. The Wolverhampton Co-operative Society served its domestic coal consumers from its Windmill Wharf Coal Yard off Stafford Road. In about 1930 Albert Fincher supervises the unloading of coal from the Cannock & Rugeley Collieries, having found a spare desk leg to prop up the wagon door, and a spare plank. (*Ralph Williams Collection*)

Road haulage made great progress between the wars as vehicles and the road system improved. Three vehicles, an Atkinson and two Fodens, belonging to Wright Brothers, line up in the late 1930s outside their depot in Crown Street. The lorries were red with black mudguards. Claude Wright stands with his dog on the extreme right. (*Claude Wright/John Spittle*)

In 1929 the Government passed legislation to make funds available for 'public works' programmes to relieve unemployment. The Great Western Railway took advantage of this to proceed with the long awaited redevelopment of its locomotive repair works at Stafford Road, on ground cut out of Dunstall Hill. Here we can see the vast 450 ft long three-bay erecting shop under construction in 1931. (*Author's Collection*)

The GWR's new locomotive repair works took over from the former works gradually, completion being in the summer of 1932. The works still looks very new when this picture was taken. As this work was completed the older premises were reorganised, and within four years the GWR had completely modernised its Wolverhampton 'factory'. In 1959 the British Transport Commission gave the first warning that the town was going to lose this major source of employment. The last stage of closure came in 1964. (*Author's Collection*)

The GWR also used the 1929 Loans & Guarantees Act to demolish the old goods depot at Victoria Basin, part of which can just be seen on the left, and to build the new Herbert Street Goods Depot in its place. Like the works at Stafford Road, it had to be brought into use while still under construction, and this picture was taken sometime between work starting in April 1930 and its completion in November 1931. Slum clearance also took place to provide land for new sidings. This shed is now used by Carver's – the building supplies merchants. (*Millennium Collection*)

Wolverhampton's industries had diversified since the 1880s, in the search of economic stability. During the inter-war years this process continued and the town was successful in attracting new enterprises such as Courtaulds, who came to Whitmore Reans in 1926, and Goodyear, who started tyre production in 1927. Here is the 'Tube Room' at Goodyear where the inner tubes for passenger service vehicles are being cured. (*Millennium Collection*)

A picture of tyre-building at Goodyear used in their own publicity. (*Jan Endean Collection*)

Supt Sidney Balance plus PCs Arthur Burge and Fred Stonier, both from the Traffic Division, and 'crowd' photographed at Goodyear in July 1929 – believed to be the occasion when the Mayor came along to see the completion of the millionth tyre! (*West Midlands Police*)

In the summer of 1936 Boulton Paul Aircraft Ltd moved from Norwich to Wolverhampton – to a site at Pendeford adjacent to the slowly developing Wolverhampton Aerodrome. The site and the workforce expanded rapidly, employing many men who had worked at Sunbeam. During the Second World War a dummy factory was also built – which failed to deceive the Luftwaffe! In this aerial view Wobaston Road can be seen on the right. (*Jack Endean Collection*)

The Midland Aero Club began flying from Pendeford in 1935, but it was not until 25 September 1938 that the Municipal Airport with its grass runways, solitary hangar and control tower was officially opened. Any municipality worth putting on the map had to have an airport, though it has to be admitted that Wolverhampton's had a fairly chequered career. A moment of glory came in the air races of the 1950s, but closure came at the end of 1970. (*Millennium Collection*)

The Sunbeam firm, established in the nineteenth century by John Marston, brought great fame to Wolverhampton's automotive industry between the wars, with the production of land speed record cars. On 29 March 1927 the 200mph barrier was broken at Daytona by Seagrave in this 1000hp 3 ton chain-driven car. It was photographed behind the Sunbeam factory, surrounded by preserved Sunbeams, and Blakenhall landmarks, on 4 July 1999. (*Ned Williams*)

Sunbeam's 'Silver Bullet' of 1930 vintage also made attempts at the land speed record but was not successful. It is seen here at the Upper Villiers Street works, Blakenhall, just before dispatch to Daytona Sands. It is posed in front of a Sunbeam car and an example of a single-deck coach built on Sunbeam's PSV chassis. (*Wolverhampton Archives*)

The Second World War

During both world wars Wolverhampton Corporation Transport recruited female staff. Amy Davies joined as a conductress in 1940, and in 1942 she passed her test to become the town's first woman trolleybus driver. In March 1967 she had the distinction of also being the town's last woman trolleybus driver. (*Amy Davies Collection*)

Geoff Turner left Wolverhampton Grammar School in 1936. While working, he joined the Territorial Army based at the Drill Hall in Stafford Street – part of the 6th Battalion, South Staffordshire Regiment. He is seen here in 1938 on parade in Stafford Street. Returning from camp at the end of August 1939, he was sent to Cannock where he heard that war had been declared. (*Geoff Turner Collection*)

The 6th Battalion of the South Staffordshire Regiment largely consisted of Wolverhampton lads. They went to Bordon, Hants, and prepared for embarkation to France with the British Expeditionary Force. In this picture members of the battalion are seen at Bordon with instruments that were taken to France. (*Geoff Turner Collection*)

The Germans attacked northern France in May 1940, sending the South Staffords into a retreat to Dunkirk and the famous evacuation across the Channel. While on the beach at Dunkirk, strafed by the Luftwaffe, some officers of the South Staffordshire Regiment posed for an amazing photograph. All are from Wolverhampton except the Frenchman at top left. Lt James is next to him, Capt. Salt is on the right, Capt. Tom Rutherford is front left. (*Geoff Turner Collection*)

Like many others at Dunkirk, Geoff Turner returned to France following the D-Day Invasion of June 1944. The Normandy Veterans Association was founded in 1981, and the Wolverhampton Branch was established in 1987. On 4 July 1999 a parade was held in Wolverhampton to mark the 55th anniversary of D-Day and Frank Tranter and Thomas Dunn, standard bearers, are seen here in St Peter's Square, with Tom Jones in the background. (*Ned Williams*)

On the Home Front. The Signals Group (25th Battalion, D Company) of the Home Guard based at the Boulton Paul Aircraft Factory line up at Pendeford. (*Jack Endean*)

The Gun Team of the Home Guard at Goodyear. Left to right: E. Rees, E. Rogers, J.H. Thompson, W.H. Chitty, J. Payne, A. Wainwright. Seated: L. Whitehouse, E. Shelton, F. Purchase. (*Wolverhampton Archives/Goodyear*)

Women members of the Corporation Transport Department line up in 1943. Standing, left to right: Cissie Hallam, Betty Hill, Lily Hyde, L.J. Davies, Mary Sweetman, Lily Brookes and Ann Pringle. Seated: Doris Cooper, Betty Wood, Amy Davies, B. Davies, Nancy Price and Winnie Perry. (*Amy Davies Collection*)

A shortage of public transport in urban areas and the moratorium on building such vehicles led to situations like this, where a Sunbeam trolleybus supplied to Bournemouth Corporation had to return to Wolverhampton to maintain services. Most Wolverhampton factories were working three shifts and public transport had to be available to cope with the movement of folk to and from work. (*John Hughes Collection*)

George Codd sells wartime supplies of whale meat from his market stall in Wolverhampton – hence the Vera Lynn song, 'Whale meat again . . .'. George entered the business by bringing fish to Wolverhampton area markets from Milford Haven in the 1930s. In 1936 he opened a shop in Broad Street, but his heart was in market trading. (*Eileen Codd Collection*)

Women workers at the Boulton Paul Aircraft factory were filmed and photographed for propaganda used to persuade women to go into war work, but the 'worker' in this picture of wing construction work was no Wulfrunian – she was a model brought up from London for the occasion! (*Jack Endean*)

A Boulton Paul Defiant plane was exhibited in St Peter's Gardens and at certain times people could climb aboard to work the power-operated gun turret just behind the fuselage. Note that the First World War hero, Seaman Harris, found himself in the display. The picture includes a trolleybus with white trim, to improve visibility in the black-out, and a very modern pram. (*Jan Endean Collection*)

The Wolverhampton 'Wings for Victory' Exhibition presented in the Civic Hall also emphasised the Boulton Paul contribution to the RAF. (*Jack Endean*)

Building a protective wall of sandbags around the Council Offices at Tettenhall early in the war. (*Wolverhampton Archives*)

Auxiliary Fire Service firefighters at work in what seems a very carefully composed picture taken at Red Lion Street. The vehicles are in wartime grey livery with white 'black-out' markings. (*Wolverhampton Archives*)

Wolverhampton became very cosmopolitan during the war and its facilities were much used by RAF servicemen stationed locally, white and black USAF airmen from separate camps near Bridgnorth, Polish and Czech servicemen, and the 'Free Dutch' army at Wrottesley. Here Queen Wilhelmina of the Netherlands visits the Princess Irene Brigade at Wrottesley in about 1944. (*Wolverhampton Archives*)

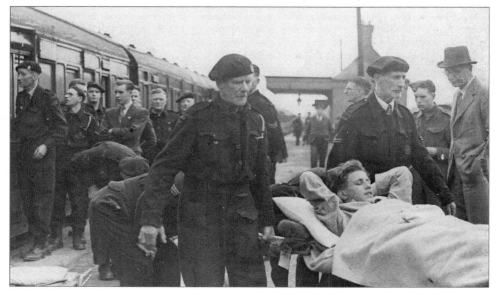

After the D-Day invasion in June 1944, the injured were flown back to Britain and dispersed by ambulance trains to selected provincial centres. Trains such as this one brought the injured to Tettenhall station, where they were unloaded by Civil Defence personnel and taken to local hospitals. This picture was taken on 6 July 1944 when the third such train had arrived at Tettenhall. (*Jack Pinfold Collection*)

VE Day celebrations: folk in Winchester Road, Fordhouses, get the flags out. (*Jack Endean*)

VE Day celebrations: folk in Uplands Avenue sit round the table. (*Anne Richardson Collection*)

VE Day celebrations: the folk in Winchester Road found some park benches and even one or two party hats. The war's over – let's have a cup of tea! (*Jack Endean*)

The Postwar Era to the '50s

May 1946 – a year after VE Day, and the Wolverhampton Co-operative Society has resumed its May Day parades. Bakery vans line up outside the Blakenhall Bakery and Mr S.H. Lewis (General Secretary) and Mrs Dale of the Management Committee line up, along with winning driver J. Hillman and his horse Peggy. (*Cynthia Stuart Collection*)

The centre of Wolverhampton, seen here in May 1947, had escaped wartime destruction and the scene remained remarkably unchanged since the 1930s (compare with page 57). Variety was still to be found on stage at the Hippodrome and the Queens was still showing films and serving afternoon tea in the café behind the balcony. Cars, consuming rationed petrol, were any colour you liked as long as it was black. (*Ken Rock Collection*)

Queen Street, looking from Dudley Street towards the station. The face of town-centre Britain was to maintain its 1930s look until the 1960s ushered in a new era of change and redevelopment. Although many shops have come and gone, H. Samuel's is still to be found at this location at the end of the century. (*Eardley-Lewis Collection*)

The war had interrupted the Co-operative Society's plans to complete a new modern 'emporium' in Lichfield Street. Its eventual modernisation after the war proceeded in piecemeal fashion. From this store the Wolves bought their football boots and Father Christmas came to compete with a man of the same name appearing at Beatties. Meanwhile S.H. 'Jack' Lewis, General Secretary, receives some lessons on what the postwar woman might expect from the CWS Desbeau corset, from Mrs Dale. (*Cynthia Stuart Collection*)

The Co-op claimed to have introduced the new concept of 'Self-Service' to Wolverhampton, and S.H. 'Jack' Lewis is seen inspecting the proceedings on 21 March 1949 at the Pendeford Lane store. This was the first of fifteen shops to be converted, although, as can be seen, conversion meant utilising existing shelves and simply removing counters. (*Cynthia Stuart Collection*)

Shortages and rationing dominated postwar retailing and the limited stock on display in shops contrasts with the overflowing shelves in acres of modern supermarket floor space. Mr Preece's shop at Collingwood Road, Low Hill, still looks smart with its new stainless steel lettering and simple frontage. (*Alice Preece*)

Whatever the stock, everyone's memory of retailing in this period focuses on personal service and 'service with a smile' – as seen in this picture of the interior of Mr Preece's shop at Collingwood Road. Mr Preece went on to be a Mayor of Wolverhampton in 1963–4. (*Alice Preece*)

How did we look now that the war was over? Ladies who had been members of the YWCA still met for tea at The Lindens – and kept their hats and coats on when doing so. Back row, left to right: Mrs Howe and three unidentified. Middle row: unknown followed by Hilda Bellingham, Alice Fallon and Mrs Oseo. Front row: Mrs Carrier, whose son became a well-known local estate agent, Mrs Hayward and Mrs Gregory. (*Anne Richardson Collection*)

Not many Wulfrunians took a camera to work to record details of their daily lives in the postwar era, but Paddy Powderley who worked for the GWR at Stafford Road did so and took this snap of his mates just outside the works. On the right is the Institute building which became quite a landmark on the Stafford Road. (*Joan Powderley's Collection*)

Another person who took her camera to work to record daily life was Marjorie Bowman, who worked in the Central Cash Office at the Co-op Emporium in Lichfield Street. In this instance, on 3 December 1955, she handed the camera to a colleague and thus appears on the left of the picture, along with Eileen Jones and Maisie Kearns. The vacuum-operated cash carrier linked the office to every department of the store. (*Marjorie Bowman*)

Women who had acquired work in local factories during the war made sure that their position was retained in Wolverhampton's postwar labour force. Here we see bicycle gear wheels being assembled at Villiers' Marston Road factory in the early '50s. The firm was a major supplier of wheels and motor-cycle engines to other manufacturers. (*Author's Collection*)

As a result of the 1944 Education Act, postwar reforms were to include the provision of part-time further education for young people who had entered the world of work. Few employers were keen to provide day-release at first, but Courtaulds and the Post Office set a good example in Wolverhampton and provided the first students for what was to become Wulfrun College in 1949. Early days in this venture were centred at The Mount, and here we see Mr Potter on 6 November 1947 leading a discussion group. (*Wulfrun College Archive*)

The Courtaulds Girls received a general education at The Mount, and in this 1947 picture Madge Cockerill, Ivy Jones and Mavis Pountney meet Mr Gray, Conductor of the City of Birmingham Orchestra, and the French horn player. Liberal education of this sort became a feature of day-release training until swept away in the 1980s. (*Wulfrun College Archive*)

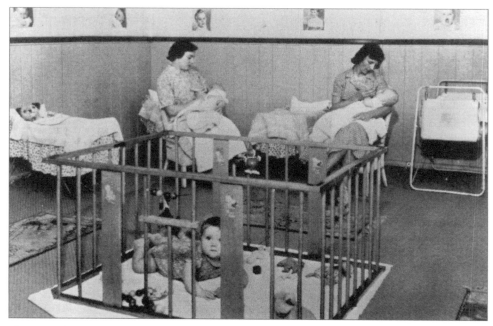

The new Welfare State established in postwar Britain set out to provide care wherever it was needed from the cradle to the grave. In Wolverhampton, as elsewhere, local government undertook new responsibilities. At New Cross where there had once been a workhouse, and then 'cottage homes' for children in local authority care, there were now 'nurseries' under the watchful eye of the Children Committee. (*Author's Collection*)

In 1948 – Wolverhampton's centenary as a Borough – the Council combined the Children Committee with the Welfare Committee to form Social Services. Some of the work previously done by the Health Committee also came under Social Services. In the following years residential homes for the elderly were built. This picture was taken at Bromley House on the Penn Road – 'for aged women'. (*Authors' Collection*)

How did we look in the early 1950s? Teenagers hadn't been invented yet so couples at the Municipal Baths on 20 October 1952 came dressed for Old Tyme dancing. The event was put on by the Gay Edwardians Dancing Club and for 3s 6d, paid at the door, you could dance till midnight to John Matthews and His Ballroom Orchestra. Couples include the Fishers, Fallons, Perrys, Holmes and Jacksons. (*Anne Richardson Collection*)

Queen Elizabeth II's Coronation in 1953 seemed to mark the beginning of a new era in which the Second World War and its effects began to be consigned to the past. In this respect it was more successful than the Festival of Britain in 1951. Both national events were celebrated locally, and the Coronation inspired putting out the flags – as seen here in Stafford Road where the staff of Charles Warner's shop enjoyed the occasion. (*Tony and Dorothy Warner*)

We return to Lea Road for a typical late 1950s street scene (compare with page 46). The trolleybuses still glided down uncongested streets – no. 444 seen here was supplied new in 1947. Some Afro-Caribbean faces are now to be seen in Wolverhampton – a town with a remarkable mix of incomers. (*the late Osmond Wildsmith*)

Although Wolverhampton's trolleybus system had remained fairly unchanged since pre-war days, some expansion did take place in the 1950s. The Wednesfield route was extended on 10 January 1955 to a new turning circle seen here at Linthouse Lane (The Albion). Such extensions reflected housing developments like those at Ashmore Park, where Wolverhampton was forced to house its 'overspill' in neighbouring territory! (*the late Osmond Wildsmith*)

Throughout the 1950s Wolverhampton's retail market was still located on the market patch between St Peter's Church and North Street – a situation that changed almost immediately in the 1960s. With the Wholesale Market nearby, and the cattle and pig market operating in Cleveland Road, close to St George's Church, Wolverhampton still seemed like a country market town until the end of this period. (*Ray Lloyd*)

The Wholesale Fruit and Vegetable Market was held responsible for causing congestion in Wulfruna Street. This 1959 picture certainly confirms that it was a busy component of the Wolverhampton scene. (*Bill Bawden*)

In the 1950s the major touring circuses each visited Wolverhampton in turn. On 7 November 1956 Billy Smart's Circus was presenting its traditional circus parade and was photographed from the Co-op in Lichfield Street as it passed the Grand Theatre. The Circus itself was built up on the Willenhall Road near the East Park Estate. (*Marjorie Bowman*)

During the same period, Pat Collins' Funfair continued to open three times a year on the Brickkiln Street patch – soon to be the home of the new retail market in the 1960s. The entrance arch faces School Street and the spire of St Mark's Church graces the skyline. In the centre of the picture Hickman's famous Boxing Show can be seen – on one of its last visits to Wolverhampton. (*Wolverhampton Archives*)

The Swinging '60s and the Sinking '70s

Wolves celebrate winning the FA Cup in 1960 by touring Wolverhampton in the team coach – provided by Don Everall Ltd, the well-known Wolverhampton coach company. Seen here the team is making its way up Broad Street. (*Phil Lycett*)

Looking down across the market patch from St Peter's Church. In the spring of 1960 an era of change was heralded in Wolverhampton by moving the market from here to the Brickkiln Street Patch. In the 1970s the Wholesale Market building was demolished, and the Courtaulds chimneys – just visible on the skyline – came down in 1973. Today the new Civic Centre fills this view. (*Bill Bawden*)

The new open retail market in 1968 – just before the stalls were modernised, photographed from the top of the multi-storey car park, then new, but demolished in 1998. St Peter's still commands the skyline but new buildings abound: the indoor market hall, the Mander Tower, the Art College and a tower-block under construction at what was still the Technical College. (*Bill Bawden*)

92

No one was in any doubt by the 1960s that teenagers had been found in Wolverhampton, as in other parts of the world. The Gaumont wholeheartedly embraced teenage musical tastes in a series of concerts that brought everyone worth knowing to Wolverhampton. The Beatles came twice in 1963, and even a scooter wouldn't get you through the resulting jams. As can be seen queues surrounded the cinema and stretched down Tempest Street. When the concert began the screams could be heard in Liverpool. (*Jan Endean Collection*)

Avril Noon, the current *Wolverhampton Chronicle* Personality Queen, met the Bachelors at Wolverhampton's Grand Theatre on 16 February 1964 when they were appearing in a variety show organised by The Water Rats. The lads have hair that is virtually touching their ears, and Avril wears hers in the current 'bouffant' style. Some found all this more challenging than the music! (*Avril Noon Collection*)

Youth culture was not monolithic in the 1960s. 'Serious' young men (and women) were followers of Traditional Jazz. Phil Bennett ran a jazz club at the Giffords Arms in Victoria Street at which the Zenith Hot Stompers were among the regular performers. Left to right: Tony Pipkin, Alan Bradley, Eric Bennett, Eddie McGrath, Alan Oliver, Norman Field and John Reade. (The last two were well-known Wulfrunians.) (*Phil Bennett's Collection*)

Every youth club in Wolverhampton produced skiffle groups and rock & roll bands galore. Giorgio & Marco's Men emanated from the St Mary and St John's Youth Club. The group also includes Peter Burn, Frank Rudge, Mick O'Dowd and Rex Walton. (*Gordon Crump Collection*)

One of Wolverhampton's premier youth clubs was the one operated at the back of St Mary's and St John's Church. Here the 'Big Boppers Rock 'n' Roll Show' is in full swing in the upstairs disco in about 1968. Gordon Crump is DJ while Sue Benfield and Sue Bampfield gyrate on the right. (*Gordon Crump Collection*)

St Mary and St John's Youth Club go ten pin bowling soon after the Bowling Alley opened on the Birmingham Road on 1 December 1964. (*Gordon Crump Collection*)

No survey of the 1960s is complete without a glimpse of Tommy Burton – seen here on the tenor sax at the Cleveland Arms in about 1962, accompanied by Phil Harris (back to camera), Mac Bailey, Trevor Worrall and Dave Holmes on drums. Tommy's contribution to culture in Wolverhampton extends from rock & roll in what had been the 'Smack' cinema in Wednesfield to his sojourn at the Lord Raglan. (*Trevor Worrall Collection*)

From the late 1960s onwards youth culture endlessly recycled itself as trendsetters ransacked the ideas of earlier times. Little wonder that we find a 'Teds' Night Out' at the Park Lane Transport Club in full swing in August 1977. If you wish to celebrate the Millennium rocking and rolling there is a group currently meeting at the Spring Vale Social Club to help you do it. (*Author's Collection*)

The 1960s saw great changes to the built environment and transport infrastructure. Wolverhampton's position as a railway town had been consolidated in the 1930s. Now modernisation and rationalisation began. In this picture taken in 1964 work has begun on removing the overall roof from High Level station, prior to the line being electrified – the modernising of this line leading to the eclipse of the Low Level line. (*the late Lionel J. Lee*)

The new High Level station, 26 February 1967. Locomotives 44944, of LMS ancestry, and 7029, of GWR ancestry, stand beneath the wires. As from 6 March the new electrified services began. The Low Level line began a long and sorry decline, the steam locomotive sheds and the Stafford Road works closed, services were withdrawn. Steam was not seen beneath the wires again for thirty years. (*Ralph Amos*)

The last steam locomotive to leave Stafford Road Works, no. 2859, did so on 11 February 1964 – and 115 years of locomotive repair work came to an end. Staff lined up for an unofficial photograph, while 'officialdom' within BR and within the Local Authority turned its back on preserving anything of Wolverhampton's railway heritage. (*Fred Richardson*)

The following years were marked by many transport orientated farewell occasions. On 11 September 1966 two ex-GWR pannier tank engines (9610 and 9630) were brought down from Wrexham and pose here, taking water at the doomed Low Level station on a special train to mark the impending withdrawal of the last GWR steam engines from service. (*Paul Birchill*)

The final Wolverhampton trolleybus journey was made on 5 March 1967 when this driver brought his vehicle (446) back from Dudley on the no. 58 route. Electric public transport would not be seen again in Wolverhampton for over thirty years. In the meantime the town would make dramatic changes to accommodate the internal combustion engine and the private motor car. (*Clifford Brown/ John Hughes*)

The 1960s also saw the demise of the Wolverhampton trolleybus system, accompanied by dramatic changes to the road system. On 22 June 1962 trolleybus 481 passes the Midland Counties Dairy at the junction of Penn Road and Lea Road. One year later services on these road were taken over by buses. The road was subsequently widened as the construction of the Ring Road progressed. The Dairy was demolished in 1988. (*Clifford Brown/John Hughes*)

Demolition in Darlington Street progresses in 1965 to prepare for the advance of the Ring Road. In 1960 the town faced congestion, and a ring road had been planned since the late 1930s! Construction began in 1960 between Dudley Road and Penn Road and swept round the town in phases over a twenty-six year period. The second phase from Penn Road to Chapel Ash caused the work seen here. (*Martin James*)

Roads like the Stafford Road, the Penn Road, and the Wednesfield Road, seen on the left in this picture, were widened – usually leaving 10 per cent unwidened just to make life interesting. At the same time new estates and tower blocks were built to provide modern municipal housing. The Heath Town development fills this 1968 picture; it was opened by Princess Margaret in April 1969. (*Bill Bawden*)

Within the town centre new precinct-based shopping was provided by the Mander Centre and Wulfrun Centre, both incorporating massive multi-level car parking. The 1960s saw the beginning of the demise of local family businesses and the commencement of a revolution in retailing. In this 1968 view of the new Mander Centre some premises are not yet tenanted, but the Barbara Hepworth statue has begun its long life of being ignored. (*Bill Bawden*)

The Mander Centre was a private venture, and was followed by the development of the Wulfrun Centre – a partnership between the Local Council and the Hammerson Group. In the end both centres satisfactorily joined up, but have remained independent of each other. They completely changed the centre of Wolverhampton in every way, and have subsequently been modernised to help the town maintain its position as a retailing centre. (*Ned Williams*)

Following the construction of the Ring Road other roads that fed into it were improved. The A449 axis had long been a candidate for widening, but such work entailed much demolition of property in Dunstall and Graisley. Millie Devitt and her brother Norman Cliff stand outside their antique and reproduction furniture shop at 33/34 Penn Road just before leaving it in 1971, followed by its demolition. This building and the doctors' surgery beyond can be seen in the background of the picture on page 24. (*Anne Richardson Collection*)

Peter Lind & Co. won the contract for widening this section of the Penn Road, photographed from the Ring Road island in about 1974, looking past Carol's and the Dairy towards the Royal School. (*Author's Collection*)

Modern Times

In the 1980s and '90s Paula Woof spent almost a decade painting a series of murals depicting the history of Wolverhampton. Her work is now displayed on the walls of the footbridge at Wolverhampton railway station. (*Wolverhampton Ad News*)

The last children's cinema matinée show in the area – the 'Saturday morning flicks' – was presented at the Odeon, Skinner Street, on 12 July 1980. Manager Colin Hunter sells the last ticket from the paybox. Shows had been running every Saturday since 1944. The cinema itself closed three years later. (*Ned Williams*)

The council gave permission for Adams Road, Finchfield, to be closed to traffic on 29 July 1981 for a street party to be held to celebrate the marriage of Prince Charles and Lady Diana Spencer. It was a traditional street party with games, dancing and singing, and here we see Elizabeth and Caroline Richardson tucking into the sandwiches. (*Anne Richardson*)

In the 1980s Wolverhampton seemed to wake up to the fact that recession and de-industrialisation were realities. Local businesses were closing, unemployment was rising, local government seemed under attack from national government. The 1984–85 Miners Strike seemed to symbolise the demand for a right to work versus government policies that regarded unemployment as a price to be paid for 'modernisation'. Miners' wives from the Cannock coalfield appealed to Wulfrunians from tables erected in Dudley Street. (*Ned Williams*)

In the early 1980s it was useless turning to the local football club to forget the economic worries of the time. To prove that Wolverhampton was alive and well the best thing to do was organise a marathon – and what a good use for the Ring Road! The eventual winner, Michael Church – no. 143 – sets off in 1988, the seventh and last of the first cycle of marathons organised by Billy Wilson, with various sponsors. The idea was revived in 1998. (*Wolverhampton Ad News*)

1985 provided an opportunity for Wolverhampton to put on a brave face and celebrate its own millennium – a thousand years since King Aethelred had granted local land to Lady Wulfruna. A programme of events was drawn up to promote an interest in the town's past, present and future. On 21 June 1985 the Mayor, Councillor George Howells, named a BR electric locomotive 'Wulfruna' at the station. On display is the 'Wolverhampton' nameplate from the 1910 steam locomotive and the 'Fair Rosamund' plate from the only Wolverhampton-built loco ever to carry a name. (*Ned Williams*)

Local schoolchildren pose alongside the newly named 'Wulfruna' at Wolverhampton station, 21 June 1985. (*Ned Williams*)

On 8 June 1985 Wolverhampton enjoyed the
Millennium Parade – the biggest carnival procession
ever seen in Wolverhampton, with floats entered by
local companies and voluntary organisations, together
with bands and dancers. The Mayor, Councillor George
Howells, and Mayoress take part in the procession in a
horse-drawn carriage, seen setting off down the Ring
Road. (*Derek Thom*)

There was an attempt to maintain the community spirit stimulated by the Millennium, and a carnival was
organised again the following year. On 2 August 1986 the parade passes along Lichfield Street behind an RAF
band. Such annual events did not catch on, and energy has since been directed towards an annual town show
in West Park. (*Derek Thom*)

In the mid-1980s Wolverhampton was still struggling to finish off its Ring Road, with the assistance of the West Midlands County Council. On 15 June 1986 work is seen to be progressing on the cutting that will take the road beneath Station Drive. The WMCC had also completed some restoration work on the Chubb Building seen on the left. (*Derek Thom*)

On the same day work was progressing on re-laying Lichfield Street to provide an approach to the proposed bus station. The Co-op, on the right next to the Sir Tatton Sykes, closed one year later and there was no sign that this area was to become the entertainment quarter of the Wolverhampton of the '90s. (*Derek Thom*)

Wolverhampton's Mayor for 1986–87 was Councillor Bisham Dass. The town was pleased to be the first in Britain to have an Asian mayor as a demonstration of commitment to a multi-cultural Wolverhampton. (*Wolverhampton Ad News*)

In February 1987 a young black Wulfrunian died in the shop Next while being apprehended by the police. Race relations again became an issue in Wolverhampton, at a time when urban Britain was often depicted as a hotbed of such issues. The fact that law and order issues can be confused with racial issues is perhaps something to do with the legacy of Enoch Powell. (*Wolverhampton Ad News*)

Som Raj was a photographer working for the local press when faced with the prospect of deportation. The local NUJ supported his cause, and this protest was staged on 22 March 1988 when an appeal was supposed to be heard regarding his Deportation Order. Eventually the threat of deportation was dropped and Som and his family continue to live in Wolverhampton. (*Wolverhampton Ad News*)

The fringe of the town centre seemed somewhat blighted by proximity to the Ring Road, and the period since the mid-1980s when the road was completed has been spent trying to tidy up these areas. Property at the foot of Darlington Street was in a poor state when further damaged by fire in the early 1990s. Despite many different plans for redevelopment, this area has become a car park. (*Wolverhampton Ad News*)

To celebrate its own centenary and to open new extensions to the brewery, Banks buried a time capsule/cask on 14 May 1990 at their Chapel Ash premises. Edwin Thompson, company chairman, stands with pint in hand while Joe Davies helps Len Crane lower the cask from the jib of his ex-John Thompson steam crane engine. (*Wolverhampton Ad News*)

One of the panels of Paula Woof's Wolverhampton Mural (see page 109). This one was completed in about 1993 and was sponsored by IMI Marston. The figures in the paintings are all real Wulfrunians. Left to right: Alderman Bantock, Sir Henry Seagrave and John Marston. Then comes Edward Elgar standing by a Sunbeam bicycle (he was a frequent user of Wolverhampton station!), George Dance test riding a Sunbeam motor-cycle and two members of the Marston management. (*Wolverhampton Ad News*)

After a decade of squeezing local government spending, the Government introduced new ways of making money available to local authorities provided they competed for it. 'City Challenge' schemes were a case in point – was it a challenge to get the money, or was it to be spent in a challenging way? Chris Khamis and Norman Davies, Leader of Wolverhampton Council, look pleased with the scheme as they stand on the balcony of the Civic Centre, which looks northwards across the Ring Road, the Molineux Hotel, and partly rebuilt Wolves' ground, early 1992. (*Wolverhampton Ad News*)

Towards the end of 1992 the Government's decision to decimate the coal industry re-awakened people's fear of such words as 'rationalisation', 'down-sizing' and 'redundancy'. On 24 October 1992 Wolverhampton MPs Dennis Turner and Ken Purchase lead the crowd in singing 'We Shall Overcome'. Also on St Peters steps are John Bird (then MEP), Norman Davies and Mel Chevanne-Reeves, plus representatives of Littleton Colliery and Cannon Industries' workforce. (*Ned Williams*)

On 31 July 1992 Wolverhampton enjoyed a royal visit from Diana, Princess of Wales, who opened the new Bilston Street Police Station and made contact with a number of Wulfrunians. (*Wolverhampton Ad News*)

St Peter's Church celebrated its own 1,000th birthday in 1994 and Councillors Fred Ledsam and Peter Bilson joined the Rector, John Hall Matthews, at the flower bed in St Peter's Gardens. In 1985 there had been some debate concerning whether such an event is a 'millenary' or a 'millennium', but on this occasion it was decided that the latter ought to be spelt with one 'n'! (*Wolverhampton Ad News*)

Another town centre innovation has been a street fair to add to the attractions of late-night Christmas shopping. On 25 November 1995 Lol Bishton's 'No. 2' set of Gallopers occupies a striking position in Queen Square – built up where the flower-sellers once stood outside the Queens Cinema (compare with earlier views such as page 62). (*Ned Williams*)

It was not until 1985 that Wolverhampton acquired a proper bus station, which then went through considerable alterations as bus deregulation took effect in 1986. This local version of the Crystal Palace was then built between the bus station and Station Drive, but as a disembarkation point soon became redundant! The single-decker is on the Council-supported innovative free town-centre service – designed to make places like the bus station and retail market feel closer to everything else. The photograph was taken on 7 July 1992. (*Ned Williams*)

Town Centre Management came to Wolverhampton in the 1990s, and money was spent on re-furnishing pedestrianised streets such as Dudley Street. Flower beds, trees, kiosks, street entertainers, orange badge holders' parking and a few seats all now vie with pedestrians for space. On 4 August 1997 Sue Ryder provides music on her guitar. (*Ned Williams*)

Percy Simmonds has long championed Wolverhampton in his role of self-made town crier. In Dudley Street on 12 September 1997 he is joined by Moira Law, Councillor Margaret Benton (Director of Wolverhampton Health Care Trust) and Sue Gurney, to promote Penn Hospital's Family Fun Day. (*Ned Williams*)

115

Today's young Wulfrunians will be looking after Wolverhampton as the next millennium gets under way. Josh Johnson (centre) helps Natalie Crosdale, Surean Maish, Manmohan Gopal and Jagjit Bratch (all aged 10) to plant bulbs, along with other children and adults at the Recreation Centre. (*Wolverhampton Ad News*)

Derek Anderson, Wolverhampton Council's Chief Executive, presents Certificates of Achievement to young people participating in the scheme run by the Youth Affairs Service, with Councillor Hill. (*Wolverhampton Ad News*)

Everyone is history-conscious as the Millennium approaches. Billie's of Tettenhall must be the town's oldest shop: as you can see the business was established in 457 BC, which probably accounts for the long white beard of the proprietor, photographed in December 1997. (*Ned Williams*)

Why does Wolverhampton appear in the *Guinness Book of Records*? Because it is the home of the world's oldest Wall of Death rider! Jerry Jones is the local lad who has become the world's senior death rider, and he is seen here (second from left) on Allan Forde's Wall of Death in West Park on 31 May 1998. Left to right: Allan, Jerry, Ken Wolf, and Chris Lee (who is also a Wulfrunian). (*Ned Williams*)

In November 1998 the School Street multi-storey car park was demolished. Many of the changes made to Wolverhampton in the 1960s have been reversed in the 1990s – both in the built environment and the social environment. The area from here to Snow Hill now awaits the next round of urban transformation. (*Ned Williams*)

On a wet day in autumn 1998 the wire-men proceed up the Bilston Road towards Wolverhampton in the last phases of constructing the Midland Metro. They are passing the back of the old bus depot – part of a large area awaiting redevelopment – and are heading for Wolverhampton's new whalebone bridge. (*Ned Williams*)

On 14 July 1998 the cast of the Grand Theatre's panto (*Robin Hood*) assemble in North Street for the launch of ticket sales. Left to right: Sam Kane, Linda Lusardi, John Inman and the Grumbleweeds. At the time the theatre was going through a £9million refurbishment, taking a late nineteenth-century jewel of a theatre into the twenty-first century, and reflecting a confidence in the future of Wolverhampton's town centre amenities. (*Ned Williams*)

Footballers have played a special role in the life of Wolverhampton in the twentieth century, and in 1999 Steve Bull announced, reluctantly, that he would have to retire. Here, with Councillor George Howells, he is presenting a T-shirt designed to mark his tenth season with the Wolves, to the *Wolverhampton Ad News* as a competition prize. Note the use of the town's coat of arms and motto – 'Out of Darkness Cometh Light'. (*Wolverhampton Ad News*)

119

The opening day of the Midland Metro, 31 May 1999, as trams begin running from Birmingham, through the Black Country to the heart of civilisation: Wolverhampton. Looking back to page 24, you will see that Wolverhampton both began and ended the century waiting for the trams, and the bright future they would herald. (*Ned Williams*)

On 25 April 1999 Sikhs march into West Park through the South Gate (see page 39) at the end of a long parade around Wolverhampton to mark the Vaisahki tri-centenary. People of all faiths joined the party in the park. The park celebrated its centenary in 1981 and is about to be refurbished. Long may it serve as that meeting place where Wulfrunians in their diversity enjoy the fruits of being a community. (*Ned Williams*)

Acknowledgements and Picture Credits

Over the years a number of people have generously made photographs available to me. Some of these people have passed away, but I know they provided photographs in the hope that they would be shared with others via eventual publication. Others have helped provide pictures with this particular publication in mind, and have responded to many requests for help at very short notice.

Pictures have been credited to their source. This is not the same thing as saying that the pictures were actually taken by that person – they are simply prints in that person's collection. In this situation every effort is made to fairly acknowledge the use of each photograph and respect people's proprietorial rights. The photographs can be family 'snaps', official photographs taken by institutions, press pictures and the work of commercial photographers. Some photographs, particularly in the first half of the book, have been issued as postcards, and I thank Ken Rock for generously making his postcard collection available. Some photographs were passed on to me in 1985 while participating in the celebration of the town's own Millennium. They were mainly commercial photographs that had found their way to sections of the Local Authority, and I have referred to them as the Millennium Collection.

Jan Endean of the Wolverhampton firm Eardley-Lewis has worked hard, and at great speed, in preparing prints for publication.

Many people contribute to a book such as this, and inevitably someone will be left out, but I wish to thank the following – arranged in alphabetical order:

Ralph Amos, Bill Bawden, Phil Bennett, Paul Birchill, Jim Boulton, Marjorie Bowman, Mrs Booth, Bert Bradford, Kevin Cartwright, Alex Chatwin, Les Clough, Eileen Codd, Gordon Crump, Ada Davies, Joe Davies, Richard Deeks, Simon Dewey, Jack and Jan Endean, Dave Evans, Keith Farley, Barbara Farnell, Goodyear Ltd, Reg Hespley, John Hughes, Keith Hodgkins, Martin James, F.J. Jennings, Josie Lee, L.J. Lee, Ray Lloyd, Johan van Leerzem (on behalf of Phil Lycett), Avril Noon, Cyril Parker, Joan Powderley, Alice Preece, Anne Richardson, Fred Richardson, Ken Rock, Jack Spittle, Cynthia Stuart, Derek Thom, Ron Thomas, Geoff Turner, A. Vaughan, Tony Warner, Osmond Wildsmith, Ralph Williams, Dave Whyley, Marion Winspur, Trevor Worrall, West Midlands Police, Wulfrun College, *Wolverhampton Ad News* (Pam Thomas and Christine George), the *Express & Star*, and the Wolverhampton Archives and Local Studies Department.